A NOTE TO PARENTS

When your children are ready to "step into reading," giving them the right books—and lots of them—is as crucial as giving them the right food to eat. **Step into Reading Books** present exciting stories and information reinforced with lively, colorful illustrations that make learning to read fun, satisfying, and worthwhile. They are priced so that acquiring an entire library of them is affordable. And they are beginning readers with an important difference—they're written on four levels.

Step 1 Books, with their very large type and extremely simple vocabulary, have been created for the very youngest readers. **Step 2 Books** are both longer and slightly more difficult. **Step 3 Books,** written to mid-second-grade reading levels, are for the child who has acquired even greater reading skills. **Step 4 Books** offer exciting nonfiction for the increasingly proficient reader.

Children develop at different ages. **Step into Reading Books,** with their four levels of reading, are designed to help children become good—and interested—readers *faster*. The grade levels assigned to the four steps—preschool through grade 1 for Step 1, grades 1 through 3 for Step 2, grades 2 and 3 for Step 3, and grades 2 through 4 for Step 4—are intended only as guides. Some children move through all four steps very rapidly; others climb the steps over a period of several years. These books will help your child "step into reading" in style!

To Michael
—J.D.

To my son Chris
—K.K.

Library of Congress Cataloging-in-Publication Data: Donnelly, Judy. The Titanic: lost...and found. (Step into reading. A Step 3 book) SUMMARY: A simple account of the sinking of the Titanic and the discovery of its remains many years later. 1. Titanic (Steamship)—Juvenile literature. [1. Titanic (Steamship). 2. Shipwrecks] I. Kohler, Keith, ill. II. Title. III. Series: Step into reading. Step 3 book. VM383.T53D66 1987 387.2'432 86-20402 ISBN: 0-394-88669-0 (trade); 0-394-98669-5 (lib. bdg.)

Manufactured in the United States of America   22 23 24 25 26 27 28 29 30

STEP INTO READING is a trademark of Random House, Inc.

Step into Reading

THE TITANIC

LOST...AND FOUND

By Judy Donnelly
Illustrated by Keith Kohler

A Step 3 Book

Random House 🏠 New York

Text copyright © 1987 by Judy Donnelly Gross. Illustrations copyright © 1987 by Keith Kohler. All rights reserved under International and Pan-American Copyright Conventions. Published in the United States by Random House, Inc., New York, and simultaneously in Canada by Random House of Canada Limited, Toronto.

1
The Wonder Ship

It is April 10, 1912.

The whole world is talking about an amazing new ship. Its name is the Titanic.

The ship is getting ready to leave on its first trip across the ocean. It is going all the way from England to America.

Newspapers call the Titanic "The Wonder Ship." They say it is like a floating palace. The Titanic has restaurants, a post office—even a gym with a toy camel to ride.

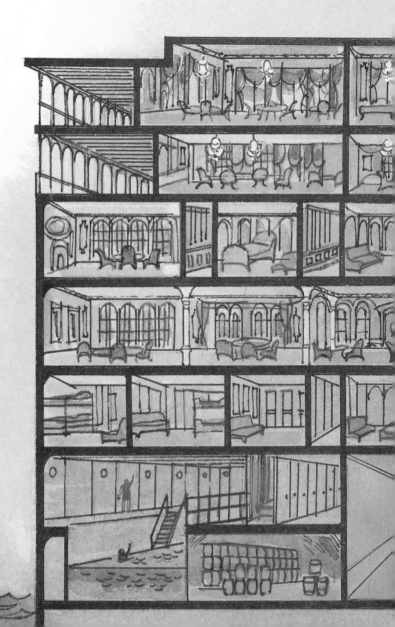

This picture shows the ship as if it were sliced open. The fancy rooms are on the top decks. On the lowest deck you can see the squash court and the swimming pool.

The Titanic is the biggest ship the world has ever seen. The ship is almost four city blocks long and is as tall as an eleven-story building.

Best of all, experts say the Titanic is the safest ship ever. They say it cannot sink. Why? The ship doesn't have one bottom—it has two. One is inside the other.

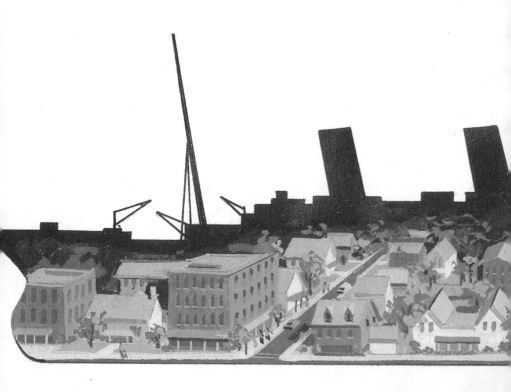

The lowest part of the Titanic is divided into sixteen watertight compartments. If one compartment starts to flood, the captain can just pull a switch. A thick steel door will shut. The water will be trapped. It cannot flood the rest of the ship. Two or three or even four compartments can be full of water. Still, the Titanic will float.

The Titanic has another nickname—
"The Rich Man's Special." Some of the
richest people in the world are sailing
on the Titanic. Their tickets cost more
money than a sailor earns in a lifetime.

Not all the passengers are rich. Some have very little money. They are not traveling for fun. They are going off to find a new home in America.

At last the big moment comes. The Titanic is ready to sail!

Crowds line the shore. Flags wave. A band is playing.

Passengers come out on the decks. They wave good-bye to their friends.

The engines roar. Slowly the ship steams out of the harbor. The Titanic has begun its first voyage.

No one guesses this will also be its last.

2
Iceberg

It is April 14, 1912. The Titanic is in icy waters off the coast of Canada.

It is almost midnight. The ship is quiet. The sea is smooth as glass. The air is biting cold.

The passengers have had a good dinner. Some of them are still up playing cards. Most are asleep in their rooms.

It is a good night to be inside. But the lookout must watch for danger. He is high above the ship in the crow's-nest. He stares into the darkness.

Suddenly the lookout sees a dark shape. It is a mountain of ice! And the Titanic is heading right into it! The lookout rings an alarm. He calls, "Iceberg straight ahead!"

A seaman is below, steering the ship. He tries to turn the ship away. But it is too late.

The giant iceberg scrapes along the side of the ship.

There is a bump. A grinding noise. It doesn't seem like much. Some people do not even notice.

But the captain hurries from his room. He goes down below. He wants to see if the ship is hurt. Soon he learns the terrible truth.

The iceberg has hurt the ship badly. Water is pouring in. Five of the watertight compartments are already flooded. And that is too many. Nothing can be done now.

It seems impossible. But it is true. The Titanic is going to sink!

The captain gives his orders. Wake
the passengers! Radio for help! And
make the lifeboats ready!

The captain is afraid. He knows that
2,227 people are on board. And there are
only enough lifeboats for 1,100 of them.

The passengers do not know this. As people come out on deck, they laugh and joke. Some are in evening gowns. Others wear life jackets over pajamas. But they are not worried. They still think they are on a ship that cannot sink.

Get in the lifeboats, the sailors tell them. Women and children go first. Men go only if there is room.

Many do not want to get in. The big ship seems so safe. The little lifeboats do not.

The sailors are in a hurry. They know there is trouble. They rush people into the lifeboats. Some are only half full, but the sailors lower them anyway.

Many passengers are far from the
lifeboats. They are the poor ones. Their
rooms are down below. They know there
is trouble too. But they do not know
where to go. A few try to find their way.
They go up stairs and down halls. Some
are helped by seamen. Most just wait
below.

In the radio room the operator calls for help. Other ships answer. But they are many, many miles away.

One ship is not far away. Its name is the Californian. This ship is only ten miles from the Titanic. It could reach the sinking ship in minutes and save everyone.

The Titanic's operator calls again and again. But the Californian does not answer. It is late at night and the ship's radio is turned off. No one on board hears the calls for help.

The Titanic tries to signal the Californian. It sets off rockets that look like fireworks. Sailors on the Californian see the rockets. But they do not understand that the Titanic is in trouble. And so they do not come.

On the Titanic the band is playing.
The music is cheerful. But people are
afraid now. The deck is slanting under
their feet.

The ship tilts more and more. The
lower decks are underwater.

Two lifeboats are left, but the sailors cannot get them loose. Hundreds and hundreds of people are still on board. And by now they know the end is near.

An old couple holds hands. The wife will not leave her husband. One man puts on his best clothes. "I will die like a gentleman," he says.

Some people jump into the icy water.
A few are lucky. They reach a lifeboat.

The people in the lifeboats row away
from the Titanic. Everyone is staring at
the beautiful ship. Its lights are sparkling.
The lively music drifts across the water.

Then the music changes. The band plays a hymn.

One end of the huge ship slides slowly into the ocean. The music stops. There is a great roaring noise. A million sparks fill the air. The other end of the ship swings straight up.

For a moment the Titanic stays pointed at the stars. Then it disappears under the black water.

3
Never Again

It is 2:20 A.M. on April 15.

The Titanic is gone.

The people in the lifeboats stare into the night. The sky is full of shooting stars. But it is dark. And it is bitter, bitter cold.

Most of the lifeboats have drifted away from each other.

People just wait. And they try to get warm. Some have fur coats. Others are wearing bathrobes and slippers. One man is in nothing but his underwear. Coldest of all are the ones who jumped from the ship and swam to a boat. Their hair and clothes are frosted with ice.

One lifeboat is upside down. About thirty men are standing on it. They lean this way and that to keep the boat from sinking. Icy waves splash against their legs.

One lifeboat goes back to try and
help. They save one man. He is floating
on a wooden door. They do not find
many others. No one can last long in the
freezing water.

Hours pass. The sky grows lighter. It seems as if help will never come. Then suddenly a light flashes. And another. It is a ship—the Carpathia. It has come from fifty-eight miles away.

Everyone waves and cheers. They make torches. They burn paper, handkerchiefs—anything. They want to make the ship see them.

The sun begins to rise. There are icebergs all around. The rescue ship almost hits one, but it turns just in time. The ship keeps heading toward the lifeboats.

Help has finally come.

All eyes are on the rescue ship. Boat
by boat, the people are taken aboard.
The sea is rough and it takes many
hours. But at last everyone is safe.

Soon the news flashes all around the world. The unsinkable Titanic has sunk. More than 2,200 people set out. Only 705 are rescued.

How? Why? No one can understand.

When the rescue ship reaches New York, forty thousand people are waiting. The Titanic survivors tell their stories.

The world learns the truth. The safest ship was not safe at all.

It was too late for the Titanic. But it was not too late for other ships.

New safety laws were passed. Many changes were made.

Today every ship must have enough lifeboats for every single passenger. And every ship has lifeboat drills so people know what to do if there is an accident.

Ship radios can never be turned off.
Every call for help is heard.

And now there is a special ice patrol.
Patrol airplanes keep track of dangerous
icebergs. They warn ships. Never again
can an iceberg take a ship by surprise.

The Titanic was a terrible loss. But
the world learned from it.

4

Found at Last

Years went by. The Titanic lay many miles down in black, icy cold water.

No divers could go down in such deep water. And no one could even find the ship. The map below shows you roughly where the Titanic sank.

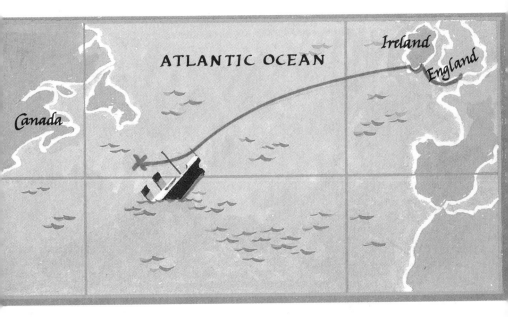

ATLANTIC OCEAN

Ireland

England

Canada

Some people thought the Titanic had been crushed. They said it was probably in a million pieces.

Yet treasure hunters kept on dreaming of the wonderful ship. They were sure there was gold on board—and diamonds and pearls.

A man named Robert Ballard dreamed of the Titanic too. Robert was a scientist. He studied the oceans.

Robert worked in a famous laboratory in Woods Hole, Massachusetts. He didn't care about treasure. He just wanted to find the ship. He thought about it for years.

Robert had a special invention. It was a kind of underwater robot. Its name was Argo.

Argo could dive down very, very deep. It had lights and a video camera. It could skim along the ocean floor. It could take underwater video pictures. And it could send them to TV screens on a ship.

Robert read all about the Titanic. He looked at maps and photos. Finally he was ready. He thought he knew where the mystery ship was waiting.

In the summer of 1985, Robert sailed north to Newfoundland. He went with a team of scientists. He took Argo with them.

Robert sent Argo hunting. He didn't even have to get his feet wet. But he had to do a lot of watching. For days it was the same. He saw sand and more sand.

Then at last something different flashed on the screen. Was it a ship? Yes, it was. A huge ship.

The other scientists began to cheer. They had done it. They had found the Titanic!

Robert could not believe his eyes. It was like seeing a ghost. There was the Titanic, sitting on the ocean floor. It had broken apart. But Robert could see how beautiful it still was.

Over the days Robert saw more and more of the ship. He saw the crow's-nest where the lookout first spotted the iceberg. A beautiful glass window lay in the sand. The ship's giant anchors were there. Bottles of wine were scattered about. And suitcases.

It was amazing. And it was sad. So many people had set out on the voyage. So few had returned.

Finally Robert sailed home. He did not tell anyone where he found the Titanic. He hoped the ship would stay just as it was. He did not want treasure hunters to come and loot it.

Robert wanted to go back to the Titanic. And a year later he did. He landed a small submarine right on the deck of the Titanic. He sent a robot inside the ship.

Robert did not take anything. But he did leave something behind. It was a message. He left it for anyone else who might find the Titanic. It asked that the great ship be left in peace.

All over the world people were thrilled by Robert's work. To some, it was very special. They had sailed on the Titanic.

They had been small children then. Now they were very old.

But they had never forgotten the "unsinkable Titanic."

The world would never forget.